THE PERFORMING PERCUSSIONIST

SERIES   Book I

JAMES COFFIN

Dedicated
to my son Marc
who decided he wanted to become a drummer!

James Coffin is Percussion Marketing Manager for Yamaha Musical Products. He was formerly assistant professor of music at the University of Northern Iowa where he received his bachelor and master of arts degrees. There he served as professor of percussion and coordinator of jazz studies. Additionally, he directed the nationally acclaimed University jazz band.

Introduction

The purpose of the Performing Percussionist series is to present the study of percussion instruments in a logical and musical manner. From the beginning, students should be encouraged to listen, think, and work on a consistent and even sound. Also from the beginning, students must concentrate on developing good "time sense" or "meter sense." These two areas - meter and sound - are stressed throughout the series.

In order to achieve the goals that have been established - meter and sound - the "right hand lead system" of sticking is recommended. This system means that the right hand is on all strong pulses within a framework of four notes: ♩ ♩ ♩ ♩ ♫ ♫ ♬♬ Using this system, students play rhythmic
R L R L   R L R L   R L R L

patterns the same way every time, thereby achieving a consistency of sound. By having a system of sticking, students learn to play rhythmic patterns quickly and increase their ability to sight-read. Another reason for advocating the "right hand lead" system is that most students will be right handed. By playing the strong pulses with the right hand and the weak pulses with the left, natural and musical accents are achieved. This type of sticking is only applicable to the snare drum. Through the use of technique studies, students will strengthen both hands. These studies are important.

The role of the percussionist in contemporary music has grown to such an extent that, early in their study, students should learn to play the accessories and the mallet keyboard instruments as well as the snare drum. Recognizing that most beginning band and orchestra literature will use primarily the snare drum, bass drum, and cymbals, the bulk of the studies in this book will be for the snare drum. However, mixed throughout the series are lessons for the accessories, with studies utilizing these instruments. By presenting multiple percussion solos in their study, students will learn to read more than one line of music. In fact, this series utilizes multiple percussion solos to teach musicianship and performance techniques. AND, THEY'RE FUN TO PLAY.

Although the series is designed for fairly rapid progress, several studies are located in the back of the book if additional work in certain areas is required.

When stressing good meter, have the students play the pulse with their right hand. Then, practice whatever rhythmic pattern they are studying, all the while feeling the pulse in the right hand. This should be done with the aid of a metronome. In fact, the constant use of a metronome is encouraged.

From the beginning, a critical analysis of performance must be established. The students must constantly listen to their playing and work for an evenness of sound.

To the Instructor

First Lesson

After the students have been shown how to set up the drum and how to grip the sticks, turn to page 6 entitled, Introductory and Daily Practice Exercises. This page should be taught by rote. The students should first count the basic exercise A out loud. After establishing the meter, they should then play and count at the same time. Stress that while practicing these daily warm-ups, the students should watch their hand positions and strive to grip the sticks correctly. Constantly make the students aware of their hand positions. Also stress meter and sound.

When the students have grasped the first set of exercises, explain how a rebound is produced. Have them rebound each stick, pointing out that the harder they strike, the quicker the rebound. Explain part B of page 6 and have them play exercises 1 and 2. REMEMBER, the hands must keep moving in a steady meter. If a rebound is missed, the students must continue playing - don't let them stop. FOR THESE FIRST REBOUND LESSONS, THE NUMBER OF BOUNCES IS NOT IMPORTANT - JUST DON'T LET THE STICKS DIE ON THE DRUM HEAD. The principle of keeping the hands moving in a steady meter while rebounding is the important lesson, not the number of rebounds.

For their first week, the students should practice Exercise A (single strokes) and 1 through 3 in Exercise B (rebounds). In other words, start them rebounding at the first lesson.

The Introductory page, or a portion of it, should be used at each lesson. At this time, correct hand positions (watching their hands), good meter, and good sound should be stressed. Exercise 4 part B is an excellent exercise for rebound warm-up.

Subsequent Lessons

It is important that the students do the written work and extra credit portion of the lessons. As they progress with their study and add rebounds to eighth notes and then to sixteenth notes, the rebounds and the hand action should get faster. At this time, have the students attempt to stop the rebound after one bounce. However, if they are unable to do so, don't force the issue. By the time they are ready for the roll studies, the only new aspect to learn will be notation.

Setting Up The Snare Drum

Fig. 1 shows the position of the snare drum stand as viewed by the student. If the traditional grip is to be used, Fig. 4, the stand should be placed so that the single brace is to the left and slightly higher. Fig. 2 shows the position of the student to the stand. When placing the snare drum on the stand, Fig. 3, first place the drum on the lower two braces and then lower it onto the single brace. Adjust the single brace so that the drum is secure. Notice that the throw-off assembly is pointed toward the student. THIS IS VERY IMPORTANT. The drum should be at least waist high when using the traditional grip, Fig. 4, with the student standing back from the drum. If the matched grip is used, Fig. 5, the drum should be lower and level. The throw-off assembly is still pointed toward the student.

Fig. 1

Fig. 2

Fig. 3

Fig. 4

Fig. 5

The Traditional Grip

Fig. 4 shows the front view of the traditional grip with the sticks resting on the drum, while Fig. 6 shows the top of the stroke, front view. The top view of the traditional grip, as viewed by the student, is seen in Fig. 7.

Right Hand

Fig. 8 shows the side view of the right hand. Note that the stick is gripped by the thumb and first joint of the index finger. The stick rests on the fleshy pads of the curled second and third fingers. The little finger may either touch the stick or rest just off the stick. The student should think of the stick as being an extension of the arm, Fig. 9. However, the butt end of the stick may rest on the heel of the hand, Fig. 10. Fig. 11 shows the side view of the right stick at the top of the stroke. Notice that the fingers are still on the stick. The top of the stroke, overhead view, is seen in Fig. 12. The student should be able to see the knuckles of the fingers, not the thumb nail.

Left Hand

Fig. 13 shows that the left stick is gripped in the crotch between the thumb and the index finger while resting on the first joint of the third finger. Both the thumb and the index finger rest lightly on the stick. The second finger is pulled away from the stick. The third and little fingers are curved naturally under the stick. Fig. 14 shows the left hand grip as seen by the student. When rebounding, the third and little fingers pull back from the stick, Fig. 15, the stick bounces, and then is caught by the same fingers, Fig. 13. The top of the left stick stroke, as viewed by the student, is shown in Fig. 16.

Fig. 6

Fig. 7

Fig. 8

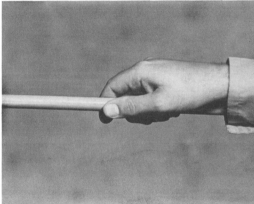

Fig. 9

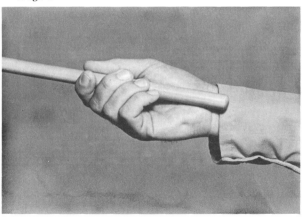

Fig. 10

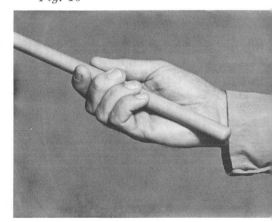

Fig. 11

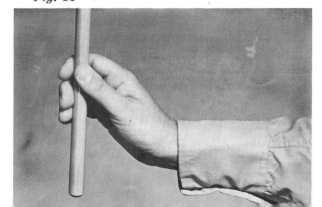

Fig. 12

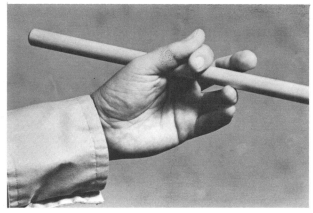

Fig. 13

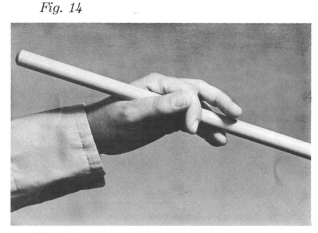

Fig. 14

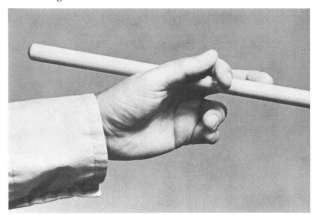

Fig. 15

Fig. 16

The Matched Grip

Fig. 5 shows the front view of the matched grip with the sticks resting on the drum, while Fig. 17 shows the top of the stroke, front view. The top view of the matched grip, as seen by the student, is shown in Fig. 18.

Right Hand

The right hand of the matched grip is the same as the traditional right hand grip. See Figures 8 - 12.

Left Hand

When using the matched grip, the left stick is held the same as the right hand. Fig. 19 shows the top of the left hand stroke.

Fig. 17

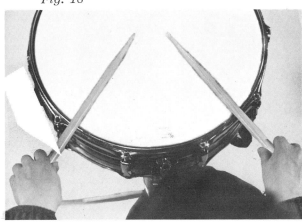

Fig. 18

REMEMBER - When striking the drum, ALWAYS DRAW THE SOUND OUT OF THE INSTRUMENT. Use a quick snap stroke. Think - down, up. Say it quickly.

Fig. 19

Because of the demands of contemporary performance and the ease of learning, the matched grip is recommended.

For beginning students, the drum sticks used should be as large as their hands will allow.

INTRODUCTORY AND DAILY PRACTICE EXERCISES

Instructor:

Teach this page by rote. Have the students use several of the exercises as daily warm-ups.

Students: While practicing these exercises watch the following things:

1. Hand positions - Refer to Pages 4 & 5
2. Stick Positions - Refer to Pages 4 & 5

Important!
How does it sound?
The strokes should sound even
Count out loud

▶ Practice with a metronome and at different tempos

Exercise A - Single Strokes

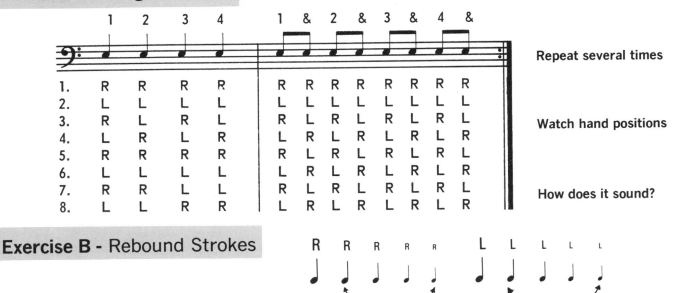

	1	2	3	4		1	&	2	&	3	&	4	&
1.	R	R	R	R		R	R	R	R	R	R	R	R
2.	L	L	L	L		L	L	L	L	L	L	L	L
3.	R	L	R	L		R	L	R	L	R	L	R	L
4.	L	R	L	R		L	R	L	R	L	R	L	R
5.	R	R	R	R		R	L	R	L	R	L	R	L
6.	L	L	L	L		L	R	L	R	L	R	L	R
7.	R	R	L	L		R	L	R	L	R	L	R	L
8.	L	L	R	R		L	R	L	R	L	R	L	R

Repeat several times

Watch hand positions

How does it sound?

Exercise B - Rebound Strokes

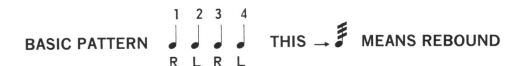

Stroke — Bounce   Stroke — Bounce

Students: While playing these exercises, always keep the hands moving in a steady tempo. If you miss a rebound (bounce) <u>Don't Stop</u> - keep the hands moving. The stick may rebound several times. Pick the stick up while it's bouncing, don't let it die (stop) on the drumhead.

BASIC PATTERN (1 2 3 4 / R L R L) THIS → MEANS REBOUND

DON'T STOP IF YOU MISS A REBOUND - KEEP THE HANDS MOVING

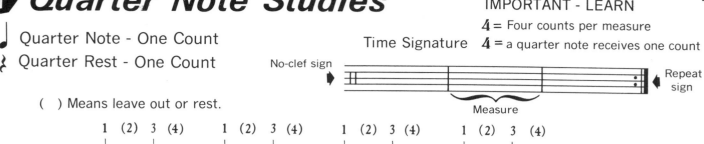

Quarter Note Studies

New · page 7

♩ Quarter Note - One Count
♩ Quarter Rest - One Count

( ) Means leave out or rest.

IMPORTANT - LEARN

4 = Four counts per measure
Time Signature 4 = a quarter note receives one count

No-clef sign → ‖ ⟶ Repeat sign

Measure

Repeat all exercises.

Keep steady tempo.

How does it sound?

Write in stickings.

Write in stickings.

WRITTEN WORK

DRAW A QUARTER NOTE.   A QUARTER REST

Extra Credit: Rebound all quarters in No. 8.

Observe all stickings - Count out loud.

More Quarter Note Studies

| DYNAMICS | *f* = LOUD | *p* = SOFT |

HALF REST: Equals — Receives 2 counts

Play all exercises to repeat sign, go back to beginning and play once more.
Do not stop at the end of the line.

1st time - Loud *f*
2nd time - Soft *p*

Write in stickings below the notes.

Observe dynamics - write in stickings for last two measures.

Write in stickings where needed.

EXTRA CREDIT - REBOUND ALL NOTES.

Watch dynamics
Practice at different speeds (tempos).

Write a half rest

How many counts does it receive? _____

Draw the sign that means Loud   Soft

WRITTEN WORK

WRITE YOUR OWN MUSIC
Use quarter notes and quarter rests.

Always play with a steady tempo - Count out loud.

FOR ADDITIONAL QUARTER NOTE STUDIES TURN TO PAGE 53

New ▶ *Eighth Notes*

Each eighth note ♪ = one-half of a count

| Two eighth notes equal one quarter note. | ♪♪ or ♫ = ♩ |

▶ YOU PLAY ALL EIGHTH NOTES TWICE AS FAST AS QUARTER NOTES ◀

Count out loud - count all eighth notes in a staccato* style.

1. Repeat many times.
2. Play correct stickings.
3. Write count above - stickings below.
5. Watch stickings.

WRITTEN WORK   Write a measure of quarter notes and a measure of eighth notes.

Write count above - stickings below.

EXTRA CREDIT: Rebound all eighth notes in Exercises 6, 7, 8, & 9.

* Short and crisp.

More Eighth Note Studies

Repeat all exercises. Play with a steady tempo

PLAY EVERY MEASURE THE SAME WAY

First Solo   SOLO FOR M.C.   Watch dynamics and use correct stickings.

EXTRA CREDIT: Rebound all eighth notes in Exercises 1 through 6

SEE IF YOU CAN MEMORIZE THE SOLO

Review Lesson No. 1

New
| %. | This sign means: Repeat the previous measure. |

MAKE SURE YOU -

1. Use correct stickings.
2. Count out loud.
3. Keep a steady tempo.
4. Watch dynamics.

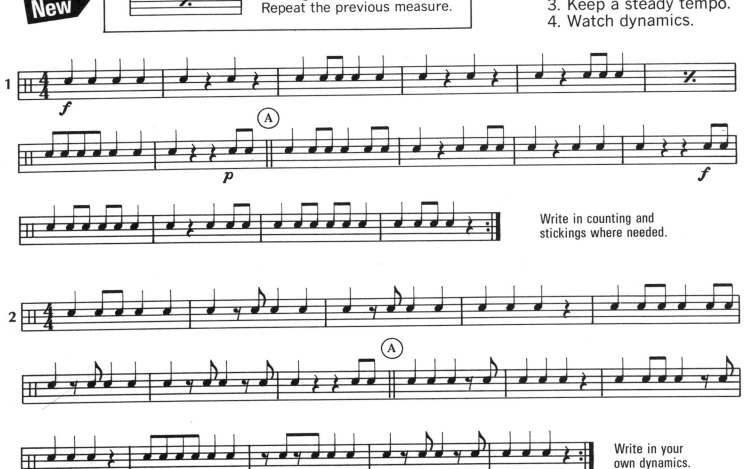

Write in counting and stickings where needed.

Write in your own dynamics.

MAKE SURE THE THROW-OFF ASSEMBLY IS POINTING TOWARD THE STUDENT.

KEY
| SNARE DRUM (SD) SNARES ON |
| TENOR DRUM (TD) or SNARES OFF |

— Snares
— Throw-off
⊗ ← Student

Two Drum Set-Up
TD SD
○ ○
⊗ Student

▶ FUN SOLO: Can be played two ways: either with two drums or one drum, using snares on and off. See box above for notation.

TUNE FOR TWO

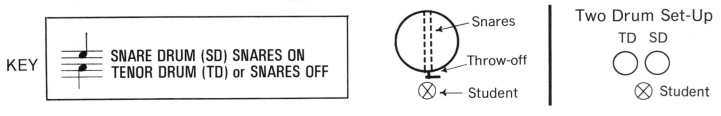

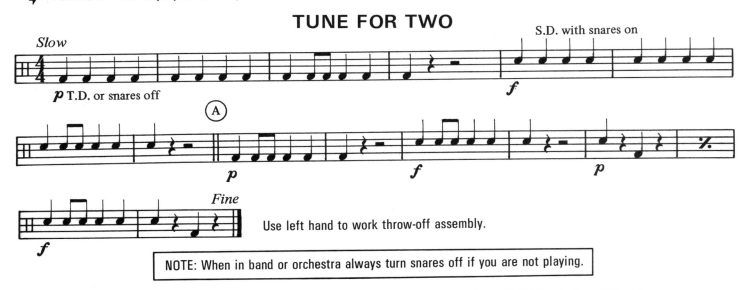

Use left hand to work throw-off assembly.

| NOTE: When in band or orchestra always turn snares off if you are not playing. |

FOR ADDITIONAL EIGHTH NOTE STUDIES, TURN TO PAGE 54

EXTRA CREDIT: REBOUND ALL 16ths IN EXERCISES 2 AND 4

More Sixteenth Notes   COUNT EVERYTHING (COUNT STACCATO)

Watch the stickings. REMEMBER: Sixteenth notes are played twice as fast as eighth notes.

▶ FEEL THE PULSE (BEAT) IN THE RIGHT HAND. USE METRONOME. ◀

Count out loud.

Make each measure sound the same.

Keep steady tempo.

Watch stickings.

Play several times.

Count out loud.

Make each measure sound the same.

Practice with a metronome.

REVIEW: Go back and play page 13 at different tempos. Keep good time, count everything and use correct stickings. Do the same with this page.

EXTRA CREDIT: REBOUND ALL 16th NOTES IN EXERCISES 9 and 10.

Review Lesson No. 2

1. Be able to count everything.
2. Use correct stickings. If in doubt look back and write them in.
3. <u>Keep a steady tempo. Use a metronome.</u>

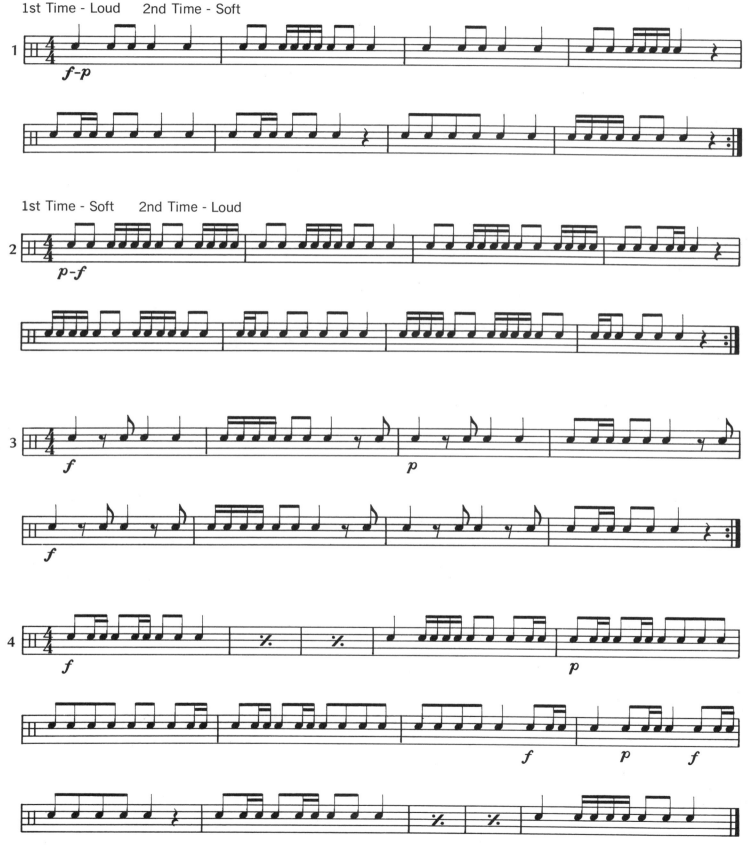

Always listen to your playing

16 More Sixteenth Note Rhythm Patterns

New ▶ ACCENTS

> ♩ This means **accent**
> (Strike a little harder)

1. Use correct stickings.
2. Count all exercises.
3. Keep steady tempo.

▶ When playing rhythm patterns that have some accented notes, play unaccented notes a little softer ◀

Dotted Eighths and Sixteenth Notes

New ▶

The dotted eighth note ♪. equals the first three sixteenth notes.
So we count 1(e&)da   Play only 1-da
              Silent   R L

Write in counting and stickings if needed.

Sixteenth Note followed by a Dotted Eighth Note

Count 1 e & da   Play only on 1 e (& da)

R L (——)   R L   Silent

Count and use correct stickings

FOR ADDITIONAL SIXTEENTH NOTE STUDIES, TURN TO PAGES 57 & 58

More Technique Exercises for Daily Practice

TO THE STUDENT

The following exercises are designed to build up your speed and endurance. While practicing, stay as relaxed as possible. The moment your arms, wrists and hands begin to feel tense, stop for awhile. By doing a few of these exercises each day, you will gradually gain more control. If you are right-handed, practice the left-hand exercises three times as much as the right-handed ones.

▶ START SLOWLY AND GRADUALLY INCREASE SPEED ◀

Basic Pattern A

1. R	L	R	L	R L R L R L R L
2. L	R	L	R	L R L R L R L R
3. R	R	R	R	R L R L R L R L
4. L	L	L	L	L R L R L R L R
5. R	L	L	L	R L R L R L R L
6. L	L	L	R	L R L R L R L R
7. R	R	L	L	R L R L R L R L
8. L	L	R	R	L R L R L R L R
9. R	R	L	R	R L R L R L R L
10. L	L	R	L	L R L R L R L R

Basic Pattern B

1. R	R R	R R R R R R R R R
2. L	L L L	L L L L L L L L L
3. R	R L R	R L R L R L R L R L
4. L	L R L	L R L R L R L R L R
5. R	R R L	L L R R L L R R L L
6. L	L L R	R R L L R R L L R R
7. R	R R L	L L R R R R L L L L
8. L	L L R	R R L L L L R R R R
9. R	R L R	R L R L L L R L L L
10. L	L R L	L R L L L L R L L L R

PRACTICE EACH EXERCISE SEVERAL TIMES. PRACTICE EACH DAY.

<u>Extra Credit</u>: After practicing Basic Pattern A, pick out one or two exercises and rebound the sixteenth notes.

TO THE INSTRUCTOR

Exercises from this technique page should be assigned in conjunction with subsequent lessons. Have the students constantly strive for more speed and control.

New ▶ *Accessories: The Triangle and the Suspended Cymbal*

An important part of percussion study is learning to perform correctly and musically the percussion accessories. The first instruments studied will be the triangle and the suspended cymbal.

Triangle

The triangle (△) should always be suspended on a piece of gut which is attached to a clamp. Either hold the triangle in the left hand, Fig. 20, or attach to a music stand, Fig. 26. NOTICE THE POSITION OF THE OPEN END. To get the purest sound from the triangle, strike on the side opposite the open end, Fig. 20. For more of a splash sound, strike the bottom side, Fig. 21. To sustain the triangle sound, rolls are produced by rapidly moving the metal beater back and forth in either one of the closed corners, Fig. 22. Rolls are notated as follows:

NOTE: Make sure that the triangle beater is the correct size for the triangle. Never strike the triangle hard, as that alters the sound. Always draw the sound out of the instrument. Unless the music states to do so, never strike the triangle with a snare drum stick.

Suspended Cymbal

The suspended cymbal ( ) may be played with either a snare drum stick or various mallets. The main hitting area is approximately 1/3 in from the edge. Occasionally, the cymbal is struck on the crown if a more staccatto sound is required. For a loud crash, strike the cymbal a glancing blow on the edge with a snare drum stick, Fig. 23. Mallets are used to produce a long sustained roll, Fig. 24. NOTICE THE PLACEMENT OF THE MALLETS. The rolls are notated the same as for the triangle: If the music

states that the cymbal is to be scraped with a triangle beater, place the beater on the cymbal near the crown and pull towards the edge, Fig. 25.

Fig. 20

Fig. 21

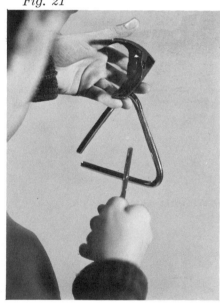

Fig. 22

Fig. 23

Fig. 24

Fig. 25

Before starting work on the multiple percussion solo, Four Sounds, learn the following:

crescendo = (cresc. ◁——————) gradually get louder

diminuendo = (dim. ————▷) gradually get softer

accelerando = (accel.) gradually get faster

ritard = (rit.) gradually get slower

mezzo forte = (mf) medium loud

l.v. = let vibrate, or let ring

(♩ = 96) a quarter note equals 96 on the metronome

(♩ = 60) a quarter note equals 60 on the metronome

Fig. 26 shows the set-up for the solo. Notice the position of the triangle and the suspended cymbal. The two drums are level, the same height, and close together. The accessories (trap) table is close to the performer. Leave the snares on throughout the performance.

Fig. 26

(the solo, Three Meters, on page 38, also uses this same set-up)

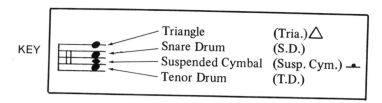

MULTIPLE PERCUSSION SOLO

KEY
- Triangle (Tria.) △
- Snare Drum (S.D.)
- Suspended Cymbal (Susp. Cym.)
- Tenor Drum (T.D.)

FOUR SOUNDS

J. A. Coffin

* At ⌢ before letter Ⓒ put Triangle beater down and pick up Snare Drum stick. Strike Triangle and Suspended Cymbal with Snare Drum stick.

 **TWO MORE NOTES**

> ♩ **Time**
> ○ Whole Note - receives 4 counts
> ♩ Half Note - receives 2 counts

Table of Note Equivalents

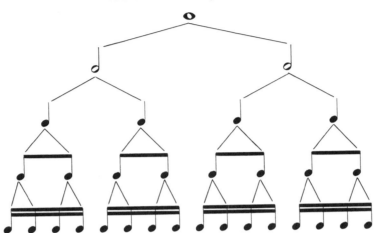

 **DOTTED NOTES**

> When a note has a dot following it, the total value of that dotted note will be: the value of the note plus one-half the value of the note.

Dotted half note ♩. = 3 counts

Dotted Quarter note ♩. = 1 1/2 counts

Dotted eighth note ♪. = 3/4 of a count

MORE RESTS

Whole Rest	▬ or ▬	Eighth Rest	♇
Half Rest	▬ or ▬	Sixteenth Rest	♇
Quarter Rest	𝄽		

WRITTEN WORK

Draw a whole note _____ it receives _____ counts

Draw a half note _____ it receives _____ counts

A dotted half note receives _____ counts. A dotted quarter note receives _____ counts.

A dotted eighth note receives _____ count.

 *Rolls*

To the Student

In order to play notes of longer duration, such as half-notes or whole notes, rolls are used. Rolls are produced by playing strokes and rebounds for the value of the notes. In previous lessons, for extra credit, you've been asked to rebound certain notes. When rebounding these notes, you've been playing rolls. Now you're going to learn various rolls and how they are used.

We have two types of rolls:

The Rudimental Roll

This roll is often called the two-beat roll or the open roll. It consists of one stroke and one rebound. If diagramed, the roll would look like this - Rr Ll Rr Ll etc.. The large notes are the strokes and the small notes are the rebounds. This roll is used on marches and when you use heavy sticks on a field drum or marching snare drum.

The Orchestral Roll

Another name for this roll is the multiple bounce roll or the closed roll. It consists of one stroke and several rebounds. Diagramed it would look like this: Rrrr Llll Rrrr Llll etc..

Once again, the large notes are the strokes and the small notes are the rebounds. The orchestral roll is used when a closed steady sound is required. As you become more experienced, you will learn what type of roll is appropriate.

To the Instructor

On page 24 is a roll study chart. It is divided into three columns. The left column contains the skeletal rhythm pattern for each roll. This pattern is made up of the number of strokes used in each roll. The middle column is the skeletal rhythm plus the rebound marking. The right hand column shows how the roll is notated. The rudimental roll listing is found at the end of each line. The correct stroke listing is bracketed. So in reality, a 5 stroke roll is really a 3 stroke roll plus rebounds.

The roll study chart should be used as a reference page. You may wish to have the students study the whole chart or divide it into sections by rolls.

At this point, the students should practice both rudimental and orchestral rolls, perhaps stressing the rudimental roll. It is very important that the students begin to control the number of rebounds. For example, don't let them play one rebound with the right hand and multiple rebounds with the left hand. The type of roll used should be consistent.

New ▶ Roll Studies

When playing rolls (rebounds) the basic rhythm pattern or SKELETAL pattern will be sixteenth notes. Rebound only sixteenth notes. When playing these exercises, keep the hands moving in a strict tempo. If a rebound is missed, DO NOT STOP. This ♪ means rebound. The right hand column shows how the rolls will be notated (written) in drum music (see note to instructor on page 23).

The stickings under the rolls in the notated column are the same as the skeletal rhythm.

* Exercise 4 can also be notated

RLRRLRR

Five Stroke Rolls - 5 (3)

The following exercises will be based upon the first four exercises on page 24

▶ Remember, each roll has a skeletal rhythm. Use correct stickings and be able to count each skeletal rhythm.

Rolls begin and end with the R. hand.

If in doubt - check on page 24

Remember ♩ and ♪ are the same.

Count and use correct stickings.

SOLO   **FRANTIC FIVES**

Nine Stroke Rolls - 9 (5)

The following exercises will be based upon exercises 5 and 6 on page 24. Use correct stickings and be able to count each skeletal rhythm.

The tie on the roll may be notated two ways.

A nine stroke roll can be notated two ways.

The end of a roll can be across a bar line.

A nine stroke roll may begin on & and will end on the next &.

SOLO

NIFTY NINES

Thirteen Stroke Rolls - 13 (7)

The following exercises will be based upon exercises 7 & 8 on page 24. Use correct stickings and be able to count each skeletal rhythm.

Remember - 13 stroke rolls may be notated either [figure] or [figure]

When the 13 stroke roll begins on &, it will end on the beat.

The roll may end across the bar line

Each roll begins and ends with the right hand. COUNT!

SOLO **TWISTY THIRTEENS**

Seventeen Stroke Rolls - 17 (9)

The following exercises will be based upon exercise 9 on page 24. Use correct stickings and be able to count each skeletal rhythm.

Remember: To be a 17 stroke roll, the half note ( ) **must** be tied to another note.

The roll may end across the bar line.

As you play the roll, keep counting the skeletal rhythm.

When the roll begins on 2, it ends on 4.

SOLO

SWINGING SEVENTEENS

Rolls of Longer Duration

Below are some examples of rolls in 4/4 time with the skeletal rhythms included.

► REMEMBER: REBOUND 16th NOTES ONLY ◄

EXERCISES USING THE ABOVE ROLLS

Rolls Reviewed   If in doubt use pages 24 and 29 as references

► BE ABLE TO COUNT SKELETAL RHYTHMS FOR ALL ROLLS ◄

At the end of Exercises 1 to 3, write the rolls used in the exercise - 5,9,13, or 17.

FOR ADDITIONAL ROLL STUDIES, TURN TO PAGE 58

 *Flams*

There are three basics you must learn to become a snare drummer.
{ 1. Single Strokes
2. Rebounds
3. Flams }

TO PLAY A FLAM, YOU STRIKE THE DRUM WITH BOTH STICKS - ALMOST AT THE SAME TIME.

Flams are notated

Right Hand Flam

The left stick strikes the drum just ahead of the right. The right is on the beat.

Left Hand Flam

The right stick strikes the drum just ahead of the left. The left is on the beat.

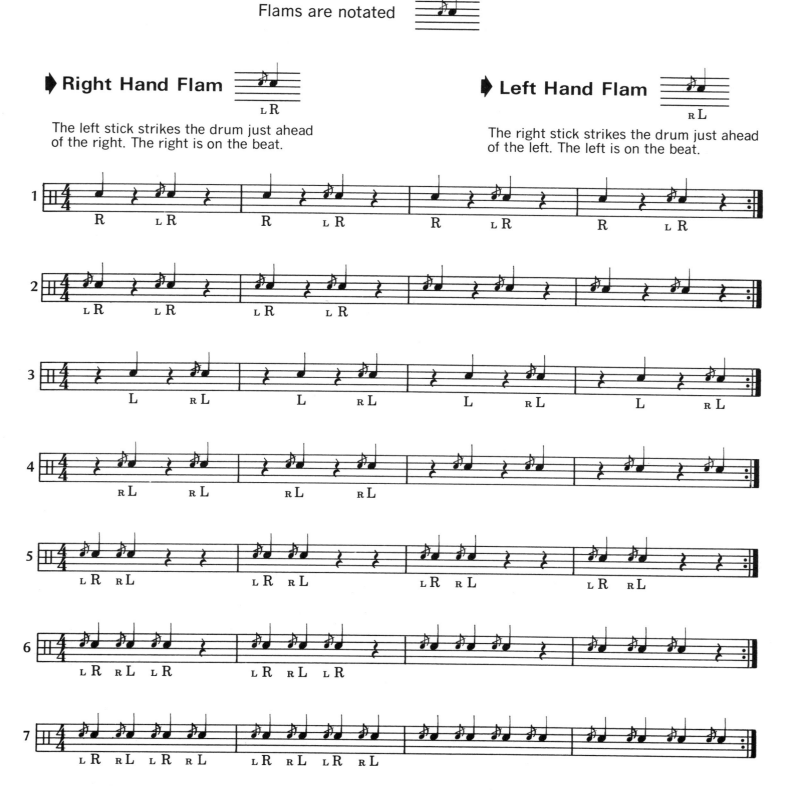

Make sure it sounds FLAM - not FA-LAM

More Flam Studies

Practice making the little note have less volume than the main note.

REMEMBER - Only use flams when they are written in the music.

Sixteenth Note Flam Studies

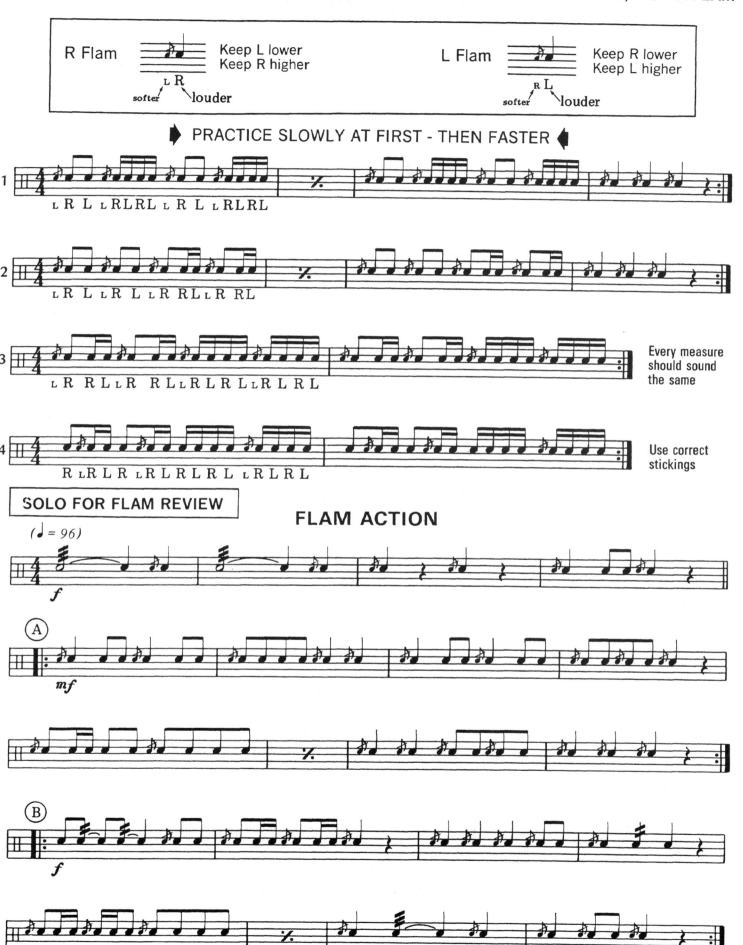

REMEMBER - FLAM, NOT FA-LAM

Go back and play all exercises on pages 31,32 & 33 using only R flams.
Notice how consistent it sounds. Practice both ways.

More Time Signatures $\frac{2}{4}$ and $\frac{3}{4}$

$\frac{2}{4}$ = Two counts per measure $\frac{2}{4}$ = A quarter note receives one count	The sticking will be the same as $\frac{4}{4}$

$\frac{3}{4}$ = Three counts per measure $\frac{3}{4}$ = A quarter note receives one count	The sticking will be the same as $\frac{4}{4}$

Measures 1 & 2
lead with R hand.

IN EXERCISE 6 USE FLAMS ON ALL OF THE QUARTER NOTES

Write some music

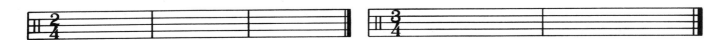

More $\frac{2}{4}$ and $\frac{3}{4}$ Studies

CHECK THE FOLLOWING
1. Stickings
2. Counting
3. Steady Tempo
4. Good Sound

$\frac{2}{4}$ *Study*

> One of the most common rhythm patterns for the snare drummer is "afterbeats" or playing "off the beat".

▶ **THREE WAYS TO STICK AFTERBEATS**

For fast afterbeats- tap R stick on R leg on the beat - L stick on the drum.

Use this for soft (p) & consistent sound.

Use this for marches.* Note - each measure begins with R. hand.

▶ **EXERCISES USING THE ABOVE PATTERNS**

Afterbeat Flams

All R hand flams - most even sound

Alternate flams- use on marches.

USE FLAM AFTERBEAT PATTERN NO. 1 FOR CONSISTENT SOUND.
USE NO. 2 FOR MILITARY MARCHES - e.g. KING, SOUSA ETC.

* Military Marches

New ▶ *Ties*

When two notes are tied together 🎵 and no roll is indicated --

do not play the second note.

Do not play!

Measures 2 and 3 are the same

Measures 2 and 3 are the same

"WALTZ"

New ▶ *Sixteenth Rests*

𝄿 In ²⁄₄ ³⁄₄ ⁴⁄₄ Receives 1/4 of a count

This is the most common use of the 𝄿 rest.

Measures 2,3,4, are the same.

SYNCOPATION STUDY

New ▶ Counting Rests

In most compositions you will not be playing
all of the time. The composer will indicate
how many measures you will <u>not</u> play like this: ⟍

This means - play 2 measures,
rest 4 measures and play 2
measures

You would count the measures of rest like this: 1-2, 2-2, 3-2, 4-2

This first number keeps track of the measures.

More examples

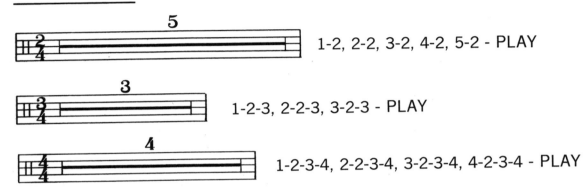

1-2, 2-2, 3-2, 4-2, 5-2 - PLAY

1-2-3, 2-2-3, 3-2-3 - PLAY

1-2-3-4, 2-2-3-4, 3-2-3-4, 4-2-3-4 - PLAY

Below is a composition using three different meters,
different instruments and measures of rest. Use the
same set-up used for the composition "Four Sounds".

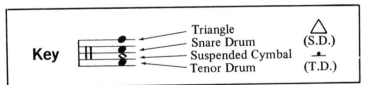

A Multiple Percussion Solo!

THREE METERS

J. A. Coffin

*Grab △ with left hand and stop sound on count 2.

New ▶ *Playing the Concert Bass Drum*

One of the most important percussion instruments is the bass drum. This drum not only provides a steady tempo on marches, but adds a deep resonant sound to the drum section. The basic bass drum tone is BOommmm - loud at the moment of impact and then gradually fading away. To achieve a more staccato sound, dampen the head with either the hand or the knee. Never tape pads on the heads or fill the drum with papers or other materials to deaden the sound. The tone must be full and resounding.

The right snare drum stick and the bass drum mallet are gripped the same way. However, the hand should be turned so that the back is down, Fig. 27.

The basic stroke is a wrist stroke, pulling the sound out of the instrument. Do not use an up and down stroke, but an in and out stroke.

The general striking area of the bass drum is approximately 1/6th the diameter of the head, Fig. 27. However, occasionally the center of the head will be struck for a more staccato sound, Fig. 28.

To dampen the concert bass drum, place the left hand on the left head opposite the striking point, Fig. 29. Or, if a shorter more staccato sound is desired the right knee will be used to dampen, Fig. 30.

To produce a sustained tone or roll, set the head into motion by playing single strokes with tympani sticks, Fig. 31, or Fig. 32.

In order to play the concert bass drum musically, thought must be given to the stroke, the hitting area, the beater or mallets used, meter, and dynamics.

The bass drum part is usually written on the bottom space of the staff with the stems down.

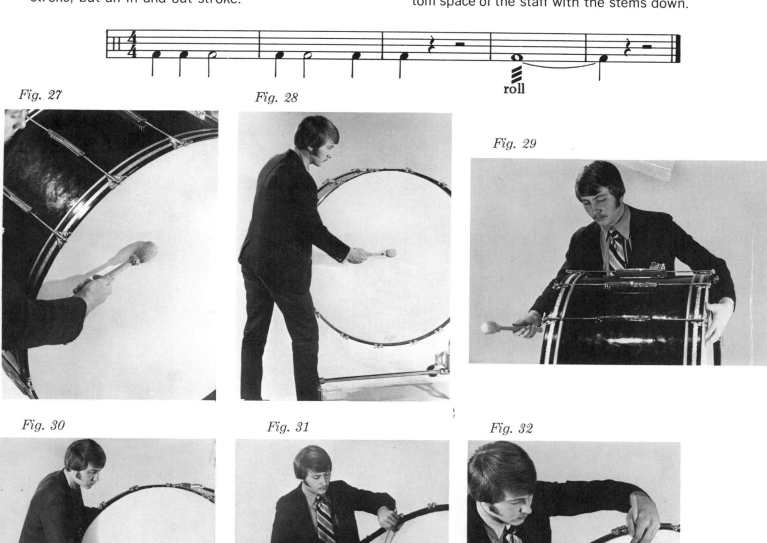

Fig. 27   Fig. 28   Fig. 29

Fig. 30   Fig. 31   Fig. 32

New ▶ *Playing the Concert Hand Cymbals*

The hand or crash cymbals add a very exciting sound to the percussion section. As with most instruments, it takes practice to perfect a good cymbal crash. In Fig. 33, the cymbals are on a stand with the straps hanging down. Fig. 34 shows the correct way to grip the cymbals. Never place your hands inside the straps.

Although there are about three basic styles of cymbal playing, the style shown here has proved to be an effective approach. As shown in Fig. 35, the left cymbal is held stationary while the leading edge of the right cymbal strikes the left cymbal, followed by the trailing edge, Fig. 36. The final position is shown in Fig. 37. The sound of the cymbals should be CA - RASH, not CRASH. Practice is needed to get the two sounds close. Never just bang the cymbals together.

Fig. 38 shows the proper style for choking a cymbal.

Cymbal music is notated several ways. Below are a few examples.

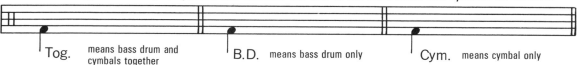

Occasionally, in marches, composers will indicate the use of the bass drum and cymbals as follows:

Tog. means bass drum and cymbals together   B.D. means bass drum only   Cym. means cymbal only

Fig. 33

Fig. 34

Fig. 35

Fig. 36

Fig. 37

Fig. 38

Marches

The drum section (snare drum, bass drum and cymbals) plays an important part in a musical composition known as a march. A military march usually follows this form: An introduction, first strain, second strain and trio. Shown below is a typical drum part for a military march.

▶ **Observe Dynamics - Listen to Sound - Use Correct Stickings - Keep Steady Tempo** ◀

MARCH APRIL

D.S. (dal segno) means go back to the sign 𝄋 and play to Fine.

---

* First and Second Endings: Play 1st ending the first time through. Repeat the strain. The second time through skip the 1st ending - play the 2nd ending and go on.

** BD 1x   Bass Drum first time.
Tog 2x   BD & Cymbals second time.

Conducting

To the Student

A most important person in any band or orchestra is the conductor. The conductor determines, from the composer's directions, how fast a composition is to be performed, how loud or soft, and whether to accelerando or ritard. So, you should always watch the conductor. If you are not sure how a part is to be played, ask your conductor before the rehearsal begins. Below are three of the standard conducting patterns. To aid you, they are diagramed two ways: first, the movement of the conductor's baton; and second, the way which you, the performer, will view the baton movements. Beat or count <u>one</u> will always be down.

Conductor

Performer's View

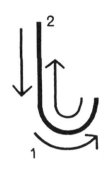 

Two-beat pattern

Conductor

Performer's View

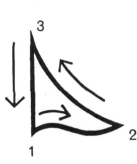 

Three-beat pattern

Conductor

Performer's View

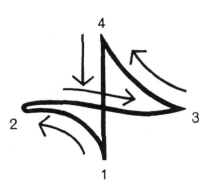 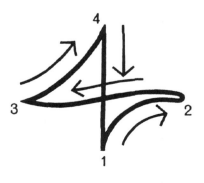

Four-beat pattern

Prior to the downbeat, the conductor will give a preparatory beat. This beat is usually in the tempo of the composition.

Conductor

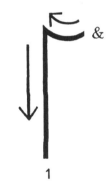

Performer's View

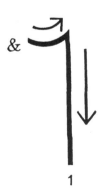

 **Duets**

The following duets may be played on two snare drums, two tenor drums, or a snare drum and a tenor drum.

COUNT YOUR OWN PART - DON'T WORRY ABOUT THE OTHER PLAYER.

Extra Credit: Play both parts at the same time. — Right Hand - Top Line / Left Hand - Bottom Line

More Duets - *Using Sixteenth Notes and Rolls*

▶ USE CORRECT STICKING, COUNT, AND LISTEN

Mallet Keyboard Studies

To the Student

The mallet keyboard instruments - xylophone, marimba, vibraharp, orchestra bells, and chimes - allows the percussionist to explore the world of melody. In this book of the Performing Percussionist series, you will study a few introductory lessons on how to play the mallet keyboard instruments. More studies are contained in Book II.

Fig. 39 shows the grip as well as the striking area of the bars. When playing the rolls, position the mallets as illustrated in Fig. 40.

REMEMBER: Playing the mallet keyboard instruments is similar to performing on other percussion instruments. Use a quick snap stroke and always draw the sound out of the instrument.

Begin by learning the names of the lines and spaces. While playing the exercises, say the note names.

Fig. 39

Fig. 40

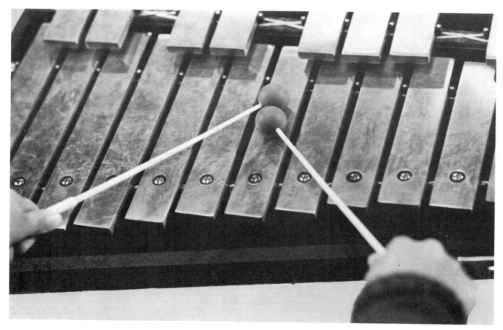

Mallet Keyboard Rolls

A mallet keyboard roll is notated like this:
To roll, single stroke rapidly on the bar. <u>No rebounds</u>
Roll for the duration of the note.

Use single strokes on rolls.

Only roll when it is so indicated.

Watch the dynamics.

SOLO   **AT PIERROT'S DOOR**

More Notes: F and G

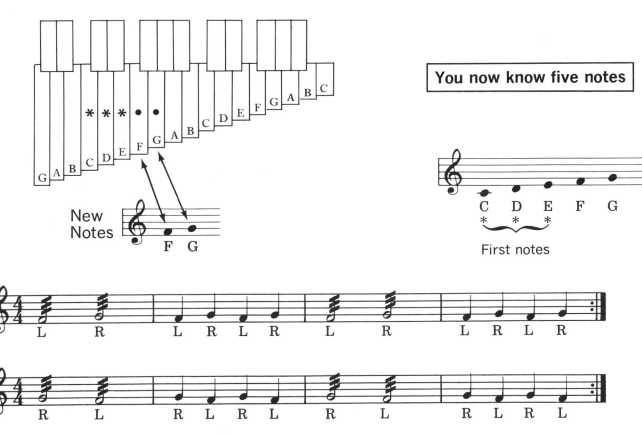

New Notes F G

You now know five notes

C D E F G

First notes

1. L R L R L R L R L R L R L R

2. R L R L R L R L R L R L

3.

L R L R L R L R L R L R L R L

Write the note names above.

4.

L R L R etc. R L R L etc.

Think the notes. Play this exercise without looking at the bars.

Performing Solo   **WALTZ FOR KIM**

Memorize this solo.

L R L R L R L R R L L

R L L R R L R L R

L R L R L L R L L R L L

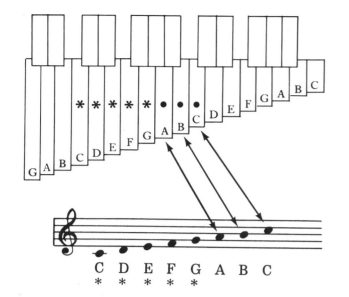

More Notes and a Scale

New

A Major Scale is made up of whole steps and half steps. It consists of seven different notes with the eighth note the same as the first, only an octave higher.

C Major Scale

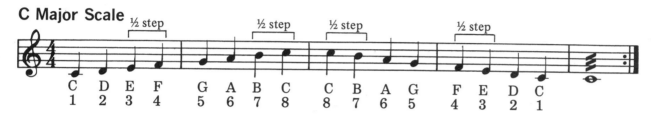

Play the above scale many times. Listen very carefully.

◆ Memorize this scale ◀

The stem on **B** may go either up or down.

Play slowly. Think the notes as you play. Listen!

New ## The C Major Chord

This is known as an arpeggio.

WRITTEN WORK

Write the C Major Scale and Chord.

Write in the note names.

C Major Melodies

Think and listen. Watch your sticking.

LITTLE MARCH

SEA WALTZ

LOOK OUT

*Strike both notes at the same time.

LAZY DAY

Additional Study
Exercises

Additional Exercises

Quarter note studies

Count - Watch stickings

1 R L R L R R L R (L) R L (RL)

R (L) R (L) (R) L (R) L

(R L) R L (R) L R L R

Use correct stickings - count out loud

2 R (L) R (L) (R) L (R) L R L R L R L R L

3 R L R (L) (R) L R L (R) L R L R R R

L L L

4

R L (R) L R L (R) L

Write in stickings

5

More Quarter Note Studies

Quarter and Eighth Note Studies

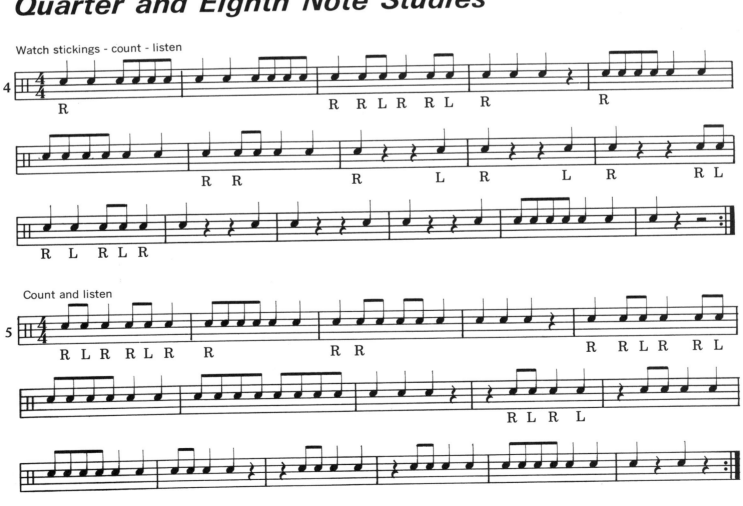

Quarter Note, Eighth Note Studies

Quter Note, Eighth Note and Eighth Rest Studies

Eighth Rest Studies

Write in counting - write in sticking.

Sixteenth Note Studies

Sixteenth Note Studies

Write in counting and sticking if needed

Roll Studies

▶ Count all skeletal rhythms. Practice using both rudimental and orchestral rolls. ◀